TEFILLIN

ARYEH KAPLAN

Published by OU/NCSY Publications,
Orthodox Union, Eleven Broadway, New York, NY 10004.
212.563.4000 • www.ou.org.

Distributed by Mesorah Publications, Inc., 4401 Second Avenue,
Brooklyn, NY 11232. Distributed in Israel by Sifriati/A. Gitler
Books, 6 Hayarkon Street, Bnai Brak 51127. Distributed in Europe
by Lehmanns, Unit E, Viking Industrial Park, Rolling Mill Road,
Jarow, NE32 3DP, England.

ISBN 1-879016-06-0

PRINTED IN THE UNITED STATES OF AMERICA

Dedicated to the memory of

חנה מרים בת בנצווין שמעל, ע״ה

whose love for Torah and mitzvos,
her family and friends,
and all of Klal Yisroel
knew no bounds.

לא יכבה בלילה נרה

A Publication

in the

JOSEPH TANENBAUM LIBRARY
Series

CONTENTS

INTRODUCTION

Hear O Israel, the L-rd is our G-d,
the L-rd is One.
And you shall love the L-rd your G-d
with all your heart,
with all your soul,
and with all your might.
And these words that I give you today
shall be on your heart.
You shall teach them to your children
and speak of them
when you are on the way
and when you are at home,
when you lie down,
and when you wake up.
And you shall bind them for a sign
upon your hand
and for Tefillin
between your eyes.
And you shall write them on the Mezuzah
of your doors and your gates.

(Deuteronomy 6:4–9)

This is the *Sh'ma*.

It is the most important part of our prayer service.

7

It is recited by every believing Jew twice each day, in the morning and at night.

It is the first thing a Jew learns as a child, and his last words before he dies.

With the possible exception of the Ten Commandments, we can say that it is the single most important passage in the entire Torah.

The *Sh'ma* contains five essential points:
1. Belief in G-d and His unity.
2. The love of G-d.
3. The obligation to repeat this lesson.
4. The commandment of Tefillin.
5. The commandment of the *Mezuzah*.

The commandment of Tefillin is repeated three other times in the Torah:

"And it shall be a sign on your hand, and a reminder between your eyes, so that G-d's Torah be on your lips; for with a strong hand G-d brought you out of Egypt." (Exodus 13:9)

"And it shall be a sign on your hand, and Tefillin between your eyes, because with a mighty hand G-d brought you out of Egypt." (*Ibid.* 19:16)

"Therefore, take these words of Mine upon your heart and upon your soul, and bind them for a sign on your hand, and for Tefillin between your eyes." (Deuteronomy 11:18)

Obviously, a commandment repeated four times in the Torah is of more than ordinary importance.

The fact that it is included in the *Sh'ma* would indicate that the commandment of Tefillin must be significant indeed.

It would pay to explore it a little further.

8

WHY TEFILLIN?

Have you ever truly loved?

Have you ever felt so close to another human being that every moment together was precious? Where every moment apart was one of longing? Where every letter and memento from this person was something to be treasured?

What if this person gave you a ring or a pin and asked you to wear it? Every time you looked at it or felt it on your finger, would it not remind you of this great love?

The greatest possible love is the love between G-d and man.

G-d told us through His prophet (Jer. 31:3), "I have loved you with an infinite world of love." To truly believe in G-d is to share this love.

To the best of our understanding, G-d's very act of creation was an act of love. It was a love so immense that the human mind cannot begin to fathom it. The Bible alludes to it, saying (Psalms 136:7), "To Him Who made the great stars, for His love is infinite."

This bond of love exists always, even when we do not deserve it. G-d is a Father Who loves His children even when they go astray. It is our duty, however, to strengthen this bond.

Tefillin are a sign of this bond of love.

Faith and love are very tenuous things. We can speak of them and think about them. But unless we do something about them, we tend to forget.

Tefillin serve to help us remember—"and a reminder between your eyes."

If you would open a pair of Tefillin, you would find that they contain four parchments. One of these parchments consists of the *Sh'ma*. It contains the commandment to love G-d: "And you shall love the L-rd your G-d, with all your heart, with all your soul, and with all your might."

This commandment speaks of three types of love. You must love G-d with your heart, your soul, and your might.

The Tefillin mirror these three aspects of love.

"With all your heart." The hand Tefillin are worn on the left hand opposite the heart. We thus dedicate our heart, the seat of life, to the love of G-d.

"With all your soul." The head Tefillin are worn next to the brain, the seat of man's soul and intellect. We thus dedicate our mind to the love of G-d.

"With all your might." The hand Tefillin are bound to the arm, the symbol of man's strength. We thus dedicate all our powers to the love of G-d.[1]

Love is the basis of the entire Torah.

The Bible therefore tells us, "they shall be for a sign . . . that G-d's Torah be on your lips."

The essence of the Torah is its commandments, *Mitzvos* in Hebrew. The word *Mitzvah* comes from a root meaning "to bind." Every commandment or *Mitzvah* serves to draw us close to G-d and strengthen this bond of love.[2]

With every *Mitzvah* we forge a spiritual bond with G-d. In the case of Tefillin, this bond is physical as well as spiritual. We literally bind G-d's love symbol to our bodies. Thus, our sages teach us that the commandment of Tefillin encompasses all others.[3] Here, we can actually see and feel the bond.

Another important theme of the Tefillin is the Exodus from Egypt—"And it shall be a sign . . . because with a strong hand G-d brought you out of Egypt." The Exodus took place over 3000 years ago. But it still plays a most important role in Judaism.

To understand the reason for this, we must realize how Judaism differs from all other religions.

Other religions begin with a single individual. He claims to have a special message and gradually gathers a following. His followers spread the word and gather converts, and a new religion is born. Virtually every world religion follows this pattern.

The only exception is Judaism.

G-d gathered an entire people, three million strong, to the foot of Mount Sinai, and proclaimed His message. Every man, woman, and child heard G-d's voice decreeing the Ten Commandments. Thus was the bond forged between G-d and Israel.

This took place just seven weeks after the Jews left Egypt. It was the climax of the drama of the Exodus.

This was an event unique in the history of mankind.

It is most important not to forget. . . .

The Torah tells us (Deut. 4:9, 10), "Be very careful and watch yourself, that you not forget the

11

things you saw with your own eyes. Do not let them pass from your minds as long as you live. Teach them to your children, and to your children's children. The day when you stood before G-d.. . ."

The parchments in the Tefillin speak of the Exodus.

The Tefillin thus serve to bind us to our past, especially to this unique event in our history.

We can understand this on a deeper level. But first we must understand the true significance of the Exodus and Sinai. We must know what it means to say that an entire people heard G-d's voice.

To hear G-d's voice is no simple matter. Only prophets hear G-d's voice. What happened at Sinai was that an entire people, men, women and children, achieved the level of prophecy.

There are many ways to approach G-d.

You can approach Him on an intellectual level. You can ask questions and seek answers until you achieve some understanding of the Infinite. This is the realm of the philosopher.

You can seek G-d on a more intimate level, in prayer and in meditation. There may then come a time when your self ceases to exist and all your senses are numbed. Suddenly, a door seems to open, if only by the slightest crack. You catch a glimpse of the Divine, and discover something more wonderful than anything on earth. Somehow you feel a unique closeness to G-d. To describe it would be as impossible as to describe the beauty of a sunset to a blind man. But you know it is there. The door has been opened to you, and you have peered through the crack.

This is the level of the mystic.

But sometimes the door is opened all the way. A man experiences more than merely a glimpse. He hears a clear voice and receives a lucid message. This is the highest possible human bond with G-d. It is the level of the prophet.

At Sinai, every Jew attained this level.

Tefillin bring us back to this unique moment.

Not many of us can be philosophers. Very few of us can attain the level of the mystic. Prophets no longer walk the earth.

But we can remember. . . .

When we bind the Tefillin to our bodies, we relive the infinite bond of love that was forged at Sinai.

There were *Tzadikim*—saints—who achieved a mystical experience every time they put on Tefillin. They could feel the words of the parchments literally burning into their heart and soul.

We may never achieve this level.

But we can begin. . . . .

G-d has given us the commandment of Tefillin and clearly spelled out how to do it.

Tefillin may seem like simple boxes and straps. But they are much, much more. . . .

WHAT ARE TEFILLIN?

As we mentioned earlier, the commandment of Tefillin appears four times in the Torah.

In each case, the Torah is telling us that certain words and concepts must be bound to our arm and to our head. We understand this to mean that the entire paragraph or *Parsha* containing this commandment must be included in the Tefillin. The Tefillin therefore contain four parchments, each one containing a paragraph with the commandment of Tefillin.

From the Torah itself, we therefore understand that the Tefillin must contain the following four *Parshos* or paragraphs. We usually refer to them by their initial Hebrew word:

1. *Kadesh* (Exodus 13:1-10), containing our obligation to remember the Exodus.

2. *VeHayah Ki YeViaCha* (*Ibid.* 13:11-16), speaking of our obligation to transmit this tradition to our children.

3. The *Sh'ma* (Deut. 6:4-9), speaking of G-d's unity and our mutual bond of love.

4. *VeHaya Im Sh'moa* (*Ibid.* 11:13-21), declaring man's responsibility toward G-d.

There is one other thing that we can deduce from the Torah itself. When speaking of the hand Tefillin, the Torah calls it an *Os*—a sign—in the singular. When speaking of the head Tefillin, however, the Torah calls them *totefos*—usually translated simply as Tefillin—which is a plural word. Since the hand Tefillin is singular, all four paragraphs are written on a single parchment and put in one box. The head Tefillin, on the other hand, contains the four paragraphs written on four separate parchments and placed in four distinct boxes.

If you look carefully at a pair of Tefillin, you will notice that the one for the hand consists of a single box. The one for the head, however, is made up of four boxes pressed tightly together.

Beyond this, the Torah tells us nothing at all about the Tefillin. There is no description of them nor any hint as to how they must be made. The Torah merely outlines their contents and tells us nothing more. It is most important to realize that G-d gave us the Torah in two parts. There is the Written Torah *(Torah SheBeKesav)*, which we keep in the ark. However, there is also the Unwritten or Oral Torah *(Torah SheBaal Peh)*, consisting of the oral tradition handed down from Sinai. The Torah was not meant to be a mere book, lying on the shelf. It was meant to be part of the everyday life of an entire people. As such, it could only be transmitted by word of mouth. The Oral Torah was handed down from teacher to disciple for almost 1500 years, until the harsh Roman persecutions finally threatened to extinguish it completely. Finally, some 1700 years ago, it was written down to form the Talmud.

The Talmud itself cites Tefillin as a prime example of a case where the full description of a commandment is found only in the Oral Torah.[4]

If you think about it, you will realize that it was not necessary to write a description of Tefillin in the Torah. One need simply look at an older pair. Tefillin were worn by virtually every adult male throughout Jewish history, and they themselves provided as permanent a record as any book.

There are ten basic laws regarding Tefillin contained in the Oral Torah, given to Moses at Sinai:[5]

1. The parchments must be made of the outermost hide *(Klaf)* of a kosher animal.[6]

2. They must be written with a permanent black ink.[7]

3. The parchments must be tied shut with the hair of a kosher animal.[8]

4. They must be placed in a perfectly square leather box.[9]

5. The box of the head Tefillin must be inscribed with the Hebrew letter *Shin*. On the right side of the box, this is the usual three-headed *Shin*, while on the left side, it must have four heads.[10]

6. The boxes must have a somewhat wider base. This is called the *Titura*.[11]

7. This base must contain an opening through which the straps are passed. This is called the *Ma'abarta*.[12]

8. The boxes must be sewn closed with thread made from the veins or sinews of a kosher animal.[13]

9. The Tefillin must be bound with leather straps, dyed black on the outside.[14]

10. The strap of the head Tefillin must be tied with a knot in the shape of the Hebrew letter *Dalet*. The hand Tefillin must be tied with a knot shaped like a *Yud*.[15]

These ten laws provide us with the basic form of Tefillin as we know them. We will discuss some of the reasons for them in the final section.

It is also interesting to note that Tefillin must be made entirely of animal products. These must all come from kosher animals. There is a profound reason for this which we will also discuss later.

The Tefillin contain the three Hebrew letters, *Shin, Dalet* and *Yud,* as a part of their basic structure. These spell out G-d's name *Sh-dai,* usually translated as Almighty. This is the same Name that appears on the *Mezuzah*. The Talmud says that this Name, spelled out in the Tefillin, is alluded to in the verse (Deut. 28:10), "And the peoples of the earth shall see that G-d's Name is called upon you, and they

16

shall be awed by you." [16]

Tefillin can be made only by a duly ordained scribe or *Sofer*. There are four callings in Judaism that require ordination: that of the Rabbi, that of the *Shochet* for slaughtering kosher meat, that of the *Mohel* for ritual circumcision, and that of the *Sofer* or scribe.

Tefillin not made by such a duly ordained scribe are *posul* and unfit for use. Since such unfit Tefillin occasionally find their way to the market, particularly in Jewish gift shops, caution must be exercised in buying Tefillin. It is best to purchase Tefillin from a reliable scribe. Tefillin coming from Israel should contain a seal of certification from the Chief Rabbinate. (The seal must be removed before the Tefillin are used.)

You may have an old pair of Tefillin from your father or grandfather. There is always the possibility that the parchments may have deteriorated, and if at all possible, they should be opened and examined by an ordained scribe. The fee for this is usually very nominal. As a precautionary measure, our tradition advises that Tefillin should be checked in this way at regular intervals (at least twice during seven years).

If you cannot get to a scribe, you may use the Tefillin as long as there is no outward sign of deterioration. [17]

If you have a pair of Tefillin, put them on today. If not, buy, borrow or beg a pair, and put them on as soon as possible.

Make it a daily habit.

There are very few things in life that are more important.

USING TEFILLIN

On the day a Jewish boy reaches his thirteenth Hebrew birthday, he becomes Bar Mitzvah. It is automatic, and there is no need, as far as Jewish law is concerned, for lavish parties or elaborate synagogue rituals. Bar Mitzvah literally means "son of a commandment." From the day of his Bar Mitzvah, a boy has the duty of keeping G-d's commandments. One of the most important of these commandments is wearing Tefillin.

The first new obligation of Bar Mitzvah is putting on Tefillin for the first time. This is even more important than being called to the Torah in the synagogue.

Wearing Tefillin every day then remains a lifelong duty.

Tefillin are usually put on just before the morning prayer.

If you wear a *Tallis*, it is put on before the Tefillin.

The Tefillin are normally worn during the entire morning service.

If for any reason you cannot say the morning prayers, you should put on Tefillin anyway.

You can fulfill the commandment of Tefillin by just putting them on and immediately taking them off. It need not take more than a few minutes. If possible, you should also say the *Sh'ma* while wearing the Tefillin.

If you cannot put on Tefillin in the morning, you can do so any time of the day until dark. If you have not put them on in the morning, you may say the afternoon *Mincha* prayer wearing Tefillin.

Tefillin are never worn at night.

Tefillin are also not worn on the Sabbath nor on festivals mentioned in the Torah, such as Rosh HaShanah, Yom Kippur, Succos, Pesach or Shavuos. As regards Chol Hamoed (intermediate festival days), consult your rabbi.

Girls do not wear Tefillin, since it is a commandment having a specified time. We will discuss this in the last section.

It is customary to stand while putting on Tefillin. (Sephardic and Oriental Jews, however, put on the hand Tefillin while sitting.)

The Tefillin are put on the arm first. This is the Tefillin *shel yad* or hand Tefillin.

They are worn on the left hand. A left handed person, however, wears them on the right. If one is at all ambidexterous, a rabbinical authority must be consulted.

The *Ma'abarta* is where the strap passes through the Tefillin. This is placed on the arm closest to where the arm joins the body. The hand Tefillin is thus worn so that it appears to hang down from the strap.

The Tefillin is placed in the exact center of the biceps muscle. When you place your arm next to your body, the side of the box should touch your chest.

Before tightening the strap, you should say, "I am now about to fulfill G-d's commandment to put on Tefillin." There is also a longer declaration included in most prayer books.

You then say the blessing:

בָּרוּךְ אַתָּה ה' אֱלֹקֵינוּ מֶלֶךְ הָעוֹלָם· אֲשֶׁר
קִדְּשָׁנוּ בְּמִצְוֹתָיו וְצִוָּנוּ לְהָנִיחַ תְּפִלִּין:

Baruch Atah Ad-noy, El-henu Melech ha-Olom, Asher kidsha-nu beMitzvo-sav VeTziva-nu le-hani'ach Tefillin.

(Bless You L-rd, our G-d, King of the world, Who has made us holy with His commandments and bid us to put on Tefillin.)

The strap is then tightened by pulling it toward the right. It is customary to wind it toward the body. (Chassidic and Sephardic Jews, however, wind it away from the body.)

The strap is wound seven times around the forearm.

The black side of the straps must always be on the outside.

Now wind the strap once or twice around the palm of the hand so that it can be held.

You are now ready to put the Tefillin on your head. These are the Tefillin *shel Rosh* or head Tefillin.

The head Tefillin should be centered in the middle of the head and worn just above the hairline.

It is most important that no part of the box protrude below the hairline. You may notice some older men wearing Tefillin on their foreheads, but they are wearing them incorrectly. Although the Torah states that the head Tefillin are to be worn "between the eyes," the Oral Torah explains that this means in the middle of the head, above the hairline. If the hairline has receded, then the Tefillin should be worn just above the point of the original hairline.

21

The knot of the head Tefillin must be centered at the base of the skull, just above the hairline in back of the head.

The straps are then allowed to hang in front.

Here again, it is most important that the straps be worn with the black side out. This is especially true on the head itself.

Very long hair may make it difficult to wear the head Tefillin correctly. For this reason, some religious Jews wear their hair short.

Before tightening the straps of the head Tefillin, say the following blessing:

בָּרוּךְ אַתָּה ה׳ אֱלֹקֵינוּ מֶלֶךְ הָעוֹלָם · אֲשֶׁר קִדְּשָׁנוּ בְּמִצְוֹתָיו וְצִוָּנוּ עַל־מִצְוַת תְּפִלִין :

Baruch Atah Ad-noy, El-henu Melech ha-Olom, Asher kidsha-nu beMitzvo-sav VeTziva-nu al Mitzvas Tefillin.

(Bless You L-rd, our G-d, King of the world, Who has made us holy with His commandments, and given us the Mitzvah of Tefillin.)

Then tighten the straps and say:

בָּרוּךְ שֵׁם כְּבוֹד מַלְכוּתוֹ לְעוֹלָם וָעֶד :

Baruch Shem Kavod Malchu-so LeOlom VaEd.

(Blessed is the Name of His glorious Kingdom forever and ever.)

(Sefardim and some Chasidim omit this second blessing completely.)

You are now ready to complete the windings of the hand Tefillin. There are several customs regarding how to do this, given in figures 1–4. Most American congregations, however, follow the Ash-

22

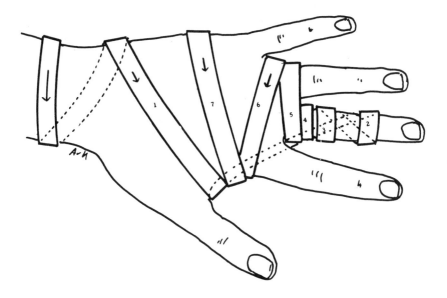

Figure 1.   Windings on Hand, Ashkenazic Custom.

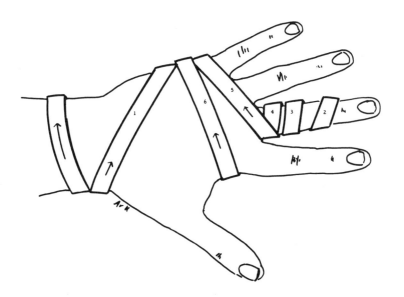

Figure 2.   Chasidic Custom.

23

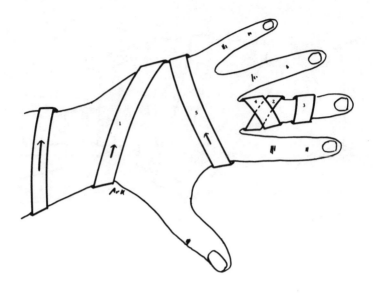

Figure 3.   Chabad (Lubavitch) Custom

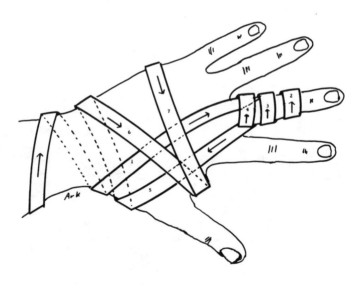

Figure 4.   Sefardic Custom.

24

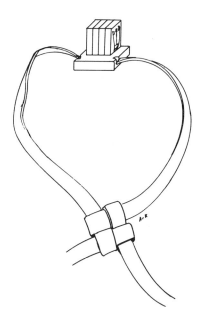

Figure 5.   Head Tefillin, Ashkenazic Custom.
Knot is in the shape of a double *Dalet.*

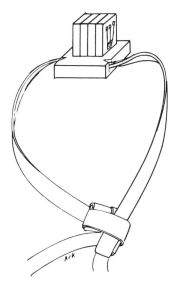

Figure 6.   Head Tefillin, Sefardic and Chasidic Custom.
Knot is in the shape of a single *Dalet.*

25

Figure 7.   Hand Tefillin, Ashkenazic Custom.
            Yud shapted knot must touch *Bayit*.

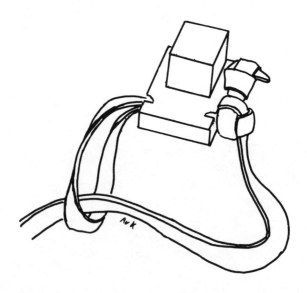

Figure 8.   Hand Tefillin, Sefardic and Chasidic Custom.

26

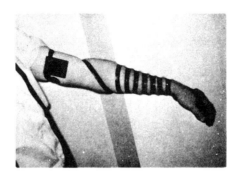

The hand Tefillin as they are worn. Note that they are in the middle of the bicep.

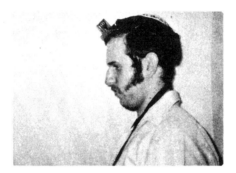

The correct positioning of the head Tefillin. Note that they are slightly above the hairline.

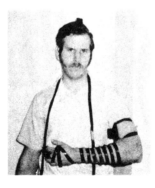

A pair of Tefillin worn according to the Ashkenazic custom.

עותבי

Tefillin worn according to the Sefardic custom.

kenazic rite, shown in figure 1, and we will discuss this in detail.

Wind the strap around your hand, passing it between your thumb and forefinger. (Winding #1)

Then wind it around the middle joint of the middle finger, and then twice around the lower joint.

The three windings around the middle finger are common to all rites, and symbolize the threefold bond of love between G-d and Israel. In a sense, they form a threefold wedding ring.

While making these windings, it is customary to repeat the following verses from the Book of Hosea (2:21–22). We are speaking to the Divine Presence of G-d:

וְאֵרַשְׂתִּיךְ לִי לְעוֹלָם· וְאֵרַשְׂתִּיךְ לִי בְּצֶדֶק וּבְמִשְׁפָּט
וּבְחֶסֶד וּבְרַחֲמִים· וְאֵרַשְׂתִּיךְ לִי בֶּאֱמוּנָה וְיָדַעַתְּ
אֶת־ה׃

I will wed You to me forever.

I will wed You to me with right and justice, with love and mercy.

I will wed You to me with faith . . . and you shall know G-d.

The windings are then completed as in figure 1.

The rest of the strap is wound around the palm of the hand (winding #7) and loosely tied so that it can stay in place without being held.

Customs vary regarding the windings on the hand, and you should follow that of your synagogue. The only requirement is the three windings around the middle finger.[18]

When you remove the Tefillin, you reverse the process. First unwind the three coils from the finger, then remove the head Tefillin, and finally take off the hand Tefillin. If you wear a *Tallis*, it is removed after the Tefillin.

You should always treat the Tefillin with the reverence due a sacred object, especially while wearing them. You should not engage in idle conversation while wearing Tefillin.

In general, it is very easy to observe the *Mitzvah* of Tefillin. It need not take more than a few minutes each day. But the true depth of this observance involves some of the most profound depths of Judaism.

We will now begin to explore these depths.

Israeli soldier wearing Tefillin at the Western Wall.

Photo by Zvi Glaser, Israel

30

A DEEPER LOOK

G-D'S TEFILLIN

Rabbi Avin bar Rav Ada said in the name of Rabbi Yitzchok, "Where do we find that G-d wears Tefillin?"

It is written (Isa. 62:8), "G-d has sworn by His right hand, and by the arm of His strength."

"His right hand" is the Torah, as it is written (Deut. 33:2), "from His right hand came a fiery law for them."

"The arm of His strenth" is Tefillin, as it is written (Psalm 29:11), "G-d gives strength to His people."

But where do we find that the Tefillin are Israel's strength?

It is written (Deut. 28:10), "And the peoples of the earth shall see that G-d's Name is called upon you, and they shall (see your strength) and be awed by you."

31

We learned that the great Rabbi Eliezer said, "This is speaking of the Tefillin on the head."

Rabbi Nachman bar Yitzchok asked Rabbi Chiyah bar Avin, "And what is written in the Tefillin of the Master of the world ?"

He replied that it contains the verse (1 Chr. 17:21), "Who is like Your people Israel, a nation one on earth, whom G-d went to redeem for Himself for a people, to make Himself a name, by great and tremendous things."

(Talmud, Berachos 6a)

It is written that G-d told Moses (Ex. 33:23), "I will take away My hand, and you will see My back, but My face shall not be seen."

Rabbi Chana bar Bizna said in the name of Rabbi Shimon Chasida, "We learn that G-d showed Moses the knot of His head Tefillin."

(Ibid. 7a)

*   *   *

We have here one of the most mysterious teachings in the entire Talmud. We are taught that G-d wears Tefillin containing the praise of the Jewish people. We are furthermore taught that when Moses asked G-d to show him the secret of divine providence, G-d showed him the knot of His Tefillin.

What does all this mean?

We know that G-d is not a material Being, and that he has neither body, shape nor form. We certainly cannot imagine Him wearing Tefillin in any physical sense.

But still, our sages were most certainly teaching us an important lesson when they say that G-d wears Tefillin. What message does this most remarkable lesson contain?

As we mentioned earlier, the commandment of Tefillin encompasses all other Mitzvos[1]. As such, it forms the basis of our understanding of all other commandments.

Somehow, this lesson appears to teach us about the relationship between G-d and the Jewish people. Exploring this concept further will lead us to a deeper insight into this relationship.

The Purpose of Creation

Why did G-d create the world?

There is a limit to how deeply we can probe, but our sages give us some insight into this question.

To the best of our understanding, G-d created the world as an act of love.[2]

It was an act of love so immense that the human mind cannot begin to fathom it. G-d created the entire world as a vehicle upon which He could bestow His good.[3]

But G-d's love is so great that any good that He bestows must be the greatest good possible. Anything less would simply not be enough.

But what is the greatest good? What is the ultimate good that G-d can bestow on His creation?

If you think about it for a moment, the answer should be obvious.

The ultimate good is G-d Himself. The greatest good that He can bestow is Himself. There is no greater good than achieving a degree of unity with the Creator Himself.

It is for this that G-d gave man the ability to resemble Himself.[4]

The first ingredient of this was free will.

Just as G-d acts as a free Being, so does man. Just as He operates without prior restraint, so does man. Just as G-d can do good as a matter of His own choice, so can man. According to many commentators, this is the meaning of man being created in the "image" of G-d.[5]

But there is another necessary ingredient.

There must be a Way to reach G-d. Only G-d Himself could provide this way.

This way is the Torah.

Thus, our sages teach us that the Torah is the blueprint of all creation.[6]

The Torah provides the means through which man can partake of the G-dly, and therefore fulfills His purpose in creation. Thus, the Psalmist said (Ps. 16:11), "You have let me know the path of life, in Your presence is the fullness of joy, in Your right hand, bliss forever."

The Torah itself says (Deut. 6:24, 25), "And G-d has commanded us to keep all these laws . . . for our good always. And it shall be righteousness for us if we keep all these *Mitzvos* before the L-rd our G-d, as He commanded us."

But there is still a third ingredient.

We need someone to follow this plan and receive G-d's goodness.

This brings us to G-d's Tefillin.

The Tefillin

In many places the Torah speaks of G-d as if He had a body. We find such anthropomorphisms as "G-d's hand" and "G-d's eye."

What does this mean?

We know that G-d is absolutely incorporeal, and has neither body, shape nor form.

But our sages teach us that G-d borrows terms from His creatures to express His relationship with the world.[7]

But what do these terms represent?

We find a hint in Elijah's introduction in the *Tikuney Zohar*[8], where he says:

Love is the right hand,
  Power is the left,
Glory is the body,
  Victory and Splendor are the two feet. . .
Wisdom is the brain,
  Understanding is the heart . . .
And the Crown of all
  is the Place where Tefillin rest . . .

G-d created the world with infinite wisdom. Thus, the Bible says (Psalms 104:24), "How great are Your works, O G-d, You made them all with wisdom."

But there is something that must come even before wisdom. There is something even higher.

What is the very first ingredient of creation? What comes even before wisdom?

The answer is purpose, and the will and desire to create.

Just as a Crown rests on top of the head, purpose and will stand above Wisdom.

The Crown of all creation is G-d's purpose.[9]

Elijah said, "The Crown of all is the place where Tefillin rest."

This means that G-d's Tefillin are intimately bound to His purpose.

In the quotation at the beginning of this section,

the Talmud asked what are in G-d's Tefillin. It answers that it contains the concept of Israel, the Jewish people.

G-d's Tefillin are His concept of Israel.[10]

When Elijah says, "the Crown of all is the place where Tefillin rest," he is saying that the concept of Israel is bound to G-d's purpose in creation.

We can readily understand this in terms of our earlier discussion. G-d's purpose in creation was to bestow good, and He created the Torah as the means through which man attains this good. Thus, the only ones who can reach the ultimate Good are those who accepted the Torah.

The ones who accepted the Torah are the Jewish people.

G-d's original purpose required someone to receive His Good. In accepting the Torah, Israel became that someone. Thus, the concept of Israel was essentially the first ingredient of creation.

This is what our sages mean when they say that the world was created for the sake of Israel.[11] It is also what is meant when they teach us, "the concept of Israel preceded all else." [12]

The Jewish people are G-d's Tefillin.

When we say that G-d wears Tefillin, we are saying that His ultimate purpose is bound up with the concept of Israel.

The straps eminate from the Tefillin and eminate to the right and to the left. This represents the two opposing forces of G-d's providence, love and strength.[13] Good comes from G-d's love, while punishment comes from His strength. These two forces come together to form the structure of G-d's justice. This is the knot of His head Tefillin.

Moses asked G-d to reveal the ultimate depth of His purpose (Ex. 33:18), "Show me, I beg, Your glory." G-d replied that such perception is beyond the power of any man (*Ibid.* 33:20), "You cannot see My face, for man cannot see Me and live." However, G-d did agree to show Moses His back, that is, the purpose underlying His justice. He thus told Moses (*Ibid.* 33:23), "I will take away My hand, and you shall see My back, but My face shall not be seen."

Our sages teach us that Moses wanted to understand the true purpose underlying G-d's justice. He asked G-d, "Why do the good suffer and the wicked prosper?" [14]

G-d then showed Moses the knot of His head Tefillin. This is where Love and Strength are bound together, forming the bond of G-d's justice.

The straps of the head Tefillin then hang down the front of the body. This indicates G-d's purpose guiding the forces of history, down to even the lowest level. But here again, G-d's purpose requires that these forces of history be intimately linked with Israel's destiny. G-d thus guides man to bring about His ultimate purpose in creation.

Thus, the Torah says (Deut. 28:10), "And the peoples of the earth shall see that G-d's Name is called upon you and shall be in awe of you." The Talmud, quoted at the beginning of this section, tells us that this refers to the Tefillin on the head. For the head Tefillin indicate that the Jewish people are the essential ingredient of all creation.

This purpose is not at all obvious. We must probe deeply before we can perceive it. This is one reason why the Tefillin are black, indicating that G-d's purpose is dark and hidden. The white parchments are only to be found when one penetrates this black barrier.

Summing up, the "place where Tefillin rest" indicates G-d's ultimate purpose.

His Tefillin are the Jewish people, uniquely bound to this purpose.

The Hand Tefillin

When we speak of G-d's hand, we are speaking of His action in the world.

G-d's hand is at work, guiding the forces of history and the destiny of each individual. Although each individual has free will, G-d guides the general course of history toward His ends.[15] The collective wills of societies are determined by G-d and governments are steered by His hand. This is what the Bible means when it says (Prov. 21:1), "The king's heart is in G-d's hand . . . He turns it wherever He wills." [16]

The ultimate goal of the historic process is the perfection of society as a vehicle for G-d's goodness.

This goal is what we call the Messianic Age, and it is the focus of the entire historical process. It is one of the basic beliefs of Judaism and gives us complete optimism in the ultimate future of mankind.

The Jewish people have a twofold role in G-d's plan.

First of all, they are His prime instruments in bringing about the perfection of this world. Through their observance of the Torah, they are able to provide an example of G-d's teachings to all mankind. Thus, G-d told His prophet (Isa. 42:6), "I the L-rd have called you . . . for a light unto the nations."

Secondly, the Messianic Age will be a time when the Jewish people will be justified before all the world. For three thousand years we have remained devoted to G-d in the face of every possible persecution and suffering. In the Messianic Age, we will be recognized as the true suffering servants of G-d.

The prophet thus said (Isa. 62:8), "G-d has sworn by His right hand, and by the arm of His strength, surely I will never again give your corn to be food for your enemies, and strangers will never again drink your wine for which you labored. But those who have garnered it shall eat it and praise G-d, and those who have gathered it shall drink it in the courts of My sanctuary."

This is a prophecy of the Messianic era.[17]

But if you look back at the Talmudic quotation at the beginning of this section, you will see that this is also the verse from which the Talmud derives the fact that G-d wears Tefillin.

The hand Tefillin indicate that Israel's destiny is uniquely bound to everything that G-d does in the world. G-d's hand is at work, guiding the world toward the realization of this destiny.

We see this in the very commandment of Tefillin. The Torah says (Ex. 19:16), "It shall be for a sign on your hand, and for Tefillin between your eyes, for with a mighty *hand*, G-d brought us out of Egypt." We have here a direct link between the Tefillin and G-d's action.

In short, G-d's Tefillin represent the Jewish people. They are worn on His head and arm, representing Israel s unique relationship to His purpose and action.

BETWEEN G-D AND MAN

It is written (Gen. 1:27), "And G-d created man in His image, in the image of G-d, He created him."

Perceive this. When a man wears Tefillin, a voice proclaims to all the angels of the Chariot who watch over prayer, "Give honor to the image of the King, the man who is wearing Tefillin."

The Torah says of this man, "G-d created man in His image."

For this man is wearing the same Tefillin as the Master of the world.

(Tikuney Zohar   47, 83b)

*   *   *

As we discussed earlier, Tefillin exemplify all the other commandments. If we can understand the meaning of Tefillin, we can perceive the deeper implication of all the other *Mitzvos* in the Torah.

We know that the Tefillin are a symbol, reminding us of our faith in G-d and of the bond of love between us. We also know that they help us recall the Exodus.

There are some who think that Tefillin are nothing more than symbols. They think the same of the other *Mitzvos.*

However, mere symbolism is not enough to explain all the detailed laws regarding Tefillin. The *Shulchan Aruch,* the main code of Jewish law, contains twenty long chapters with all the intricate rules concerning the making and wearing of Tefillin. If even a single word is misspelled or a letter deformed, the Tefillin are *posul* and absolutely useless. And this is in the parchments, which are completely hidden in the Tefillin boxes.

If it is mere symbolism, then why all this attention to detail? [18]

Why not just hang a picture of Tefillin on the wall and merely look at it?

Why not simply meditate on Tefillin and their inner meaning?

Why do we have to actually wear such intricate ritual objects?

But, as we mentioned earlier, the greatest good that G-d can offer us is our ability to approach G-d and resemble Him. When we wear Tefillin, we are projecting ourselves in the image of G-d wearing Tefillin. This is more than mere symbolism. It is an imitation of the Divine.

This is the meaning of the quotation at the beginning of this section.

The author of the *Yesod VeShoresh HaAvodah* [19] comments that this is the reason for all the detailed laws of Tefillin. Every detail of the Tefillin we wear has a counterpart in the Tefillin on high.

There are some people who find it difficult to understand how a mere physical act, such as wearing Tefillin, can bring one close to G-d. They would say that the best way to accomplish this would be through meditation and contemplation, or through philosophical speculation.

These might be helpful, but they can never bring man to this goal. G-d told His prophet (Isa. 55:9), "As the heavens are higher than the earth, so are My ways higher than your ways, and My thoughts, than your thoughts."

41

But this does not really solve the problem.

If we cannot draw close to G-d through such spiritual exercises as meditation and contemplation, how can we do it through a mere physical act such as wearing Tefillin?

In order to understand this, we must ask another simple but profound question.

Why did G-d create the physical world?

This is really a difficult question. G-d Himself is certainly spiritual, and so is the Good that He has to give. The entire purpose of creation is essentially spiritual in scope.

Then what necessity was there in creating a physical world at all?

In order to answer this question, we must ask still another question.

What is the difference between the spiritual and the physical?

We speak of the two concepts, the spiritual and the physical, and realize that there is a difference between the two. But precisely what is it?

The answer is really quite simple. The main difference between the spiritual and the physical involves the concept of space. Physical space exists only in the physical world. In the spiritual domain, there is no concept of space as we know it.

But still we speak of things being close or far apart in the spiritual world. What does this mean?

We cannot be speaking of physical distance, for there is no physical space in the spiritual realm.

But in a spiritual sense, closeness involves resemblance.[20]

Two things that resemble each other are spiritually close. On the other hand, two things that differ are far apart in a spiritual sense.

This has very important implications. In the spiritual world, it is impossible to bring two opposites together. Because they are opposites, by definition they are poles apart.

But spiritual things can be bound to the material, just as the soul is bound to the body.

Two opposites can be brought together when they are both bound to the same material object. For in the physical world we can literally push two opposites together.

Thus, for example, man has both an urge for good and an urge for evil, the *Yetzer Tov* and the *Yetzer HaRa*. In a purely spiritual sense, these are poles apart. Without the material, they could never be brought together in a single spiritual entity. It is only in a physical body that they can be brought together. Although they are at opposite poles spiritually, they come together in the physical man.[21]

G-d and man are also worlds apart—"as the heavens are higher than the earth." On a purely spiritual plane, it would be totally impossible for the two ever to be brought together. All the meditating and philosophising in the world cannot bridge this gap.

It is only here in the physical world that G-d and man can come together. In some ways, both can bind themselves to the same physical object or action. In this way, they are almost physically pushed together.

Here again, we can use Tefillin as an example.

The physical Tefillin we wear are a counterpart of the Tefillin on high. In each detail, they parallel G-d's spiritual Tefillin. And because they *resemble* these Tefillin, they are spiritually very close to them.

But as we discussed in the previous level, G-d's Tefillin are on the very Crown of creation. They exist at the very highest transcendental level.

When a man wears Tefillin, he therefore binds himself to the very highest spiritual level. He achieves a closeness to G-d that even the deepest meditation could not accomplish.

Of course, when a man wears Tefillin and also contemplates their significance, his very thoughts are elevated close to G-d. But even the physical act in itself can bring a man to the loftiest heights.

We can also understand this in a much simpler sense.

It is G-d's will that we wear Tefillin. Our physical Tefillin are therefore intimately bound to G-d's will.

But as we mentioned in the previous section, G-d's will is the Crown of existence, the very first stage in creation. Thus, our physical Tefillin are bound to the very highest transcendental level.

But when a man wears Tefillin, he is also bound to them.

Suddenly, this man has something in common with the Crown of existence. Both his body and G-d's will are intimately bound to the same physical object, in this case, Tefillin. Through the physical, he can literally push himself into contact with the G-dly.[22]

The same is true of all the other *Mitzvos.*

As we mentioned in the first section, the word *Mitzvah* comes from a root meaning "to bind." Through the physical act of doing a *Mitzvah,* we literally bind ourselves to G-d.

We can now understand the reason for all the detailed laws of Tefillin. In order to create this bond, our Tefillin must conform exactly to their counterpart on high. The slightest deviation breaks this link.

A good analogy is that of a radio. A radio is specifically designed to receive a particular type of signal. Every element in it is needed for this. Cut a single wire, remove a single capacitor, no matter how small, and you no longer receive the signal. There are precise rules by which a radio must be built. These include all the laws of electromagnetism and circuits. If these are not exactly followed, the radio will not function.

Tefillin are our receiver for a spiritual signal. As such, they must be designed to receive this particular kind of signal. Violate a single rule, and they become like a radio with a transistor removed. The bond just no longer exists.

We can carry the analogy still further. You would have to have an extensive scientific education to even begin to understand how a radio works. You would have to know calculus and differential equations and all the complexities of electromagnetic theory. But still, even the youngest child can turn on a radio.

The same is true of the *Mitzvos*. A lifetime of study might lead you to begin to understand their significance. But anyone can put them on and receive the signal.

In the following sections, we will explore the meaning of a number of rules governing Tefillin. In doing so, we must bear in mind that this is not mere symbolism, but an analogue of the very forces underlying the purpose of creation.

We must also keep in mind that everything discussed here reflects only a very small fraction of their true significance.

Let us now examine one seemingly trivial example.

BY A HAIR

G-d Himself gave existence to the side of Evil and allows it to exist.

We must therefore not take it lightly, but safeguard ourselves so that it does not denounce us.

We give the side of Evil a small place in our most holy realm. For all its power ultimately comes from the Holy.

This is the mystery of the hair of the Calf inside the Tefillin.

This hair is allowed to show on the outside, but so short as not to cause defilement.

We must bring this hair into our highest sanctuary and give it a place, in order that it not denounce us.

(Zohar, Pekudey 237b)

*   *   *

If you look carefully at the head Tefillin, you will see four very short hairs, coming out near the base, between the third and fourth sections.

In the section "What are Tefillin," we mentioned that one of the basic rules of Tefillin require that the parchments be tied with the hair of a kosher animal. The Tefillin may be perfect in every other respect, but if this hair is missing, they are *posul* and unfit for use.

It is customary to use the hair of a calf to bind the parchments. It is also necessary to pass these hairs through a small opening in the Tefillin so that they be visible on the outside. The length of hair showing on the outside is less than the length of a barleycorn.[23]

This is certainly one of the strangest rules involving Tefillin. Yet, the significance of this hair leads us to understand some of the most profound concepts of Judaism. It is intimately bound to the question of good and evil.

Again, let us begin our discussion with a question.

Why does G-d allow evil to exist? Why did He allow for the possibility of evil in the first place?

In order to understand this, we must go back to an earlier discussion. As we mentioned earlier, one of the most profound ways in which man resembles his Creator is in his possession of free will. This free will is one of the most basic ingredients of creation.

But just as man must have free will, he must also have freedom of choice. A man locked up in prison may have the same free will as anyone else, but there is little that he can do with it. For man to resemble his Creator to the greatest possible degree, he must exist in an arena where he has the maximum freedom of choice. The more man resembles G-d in His omnipotence, the closer he can resemble Him in his free choice of the good.

To make this freedom of choice real, G-d also had to create the possibility of evil.[24] If nothing but good were possible, it would produce no benefit. To use the Talmudic metaphor, it would be like carrying a lamp in broad daylight.[25]

The *Zohar* thus states, "The advantage of wisdom comes from folly, just as that of light comes from darkness. If there were no darkness, then light would not be discernable, and would produce no benefit. . . . Thus, it is written (Eccl. 7:14), 'G-d has made one thing opposite the other.' " [26]

G-d therefore told His prophet (Isa. 45:7), "I form light and create darkness, I make peace and create evil."

Originally, G-d gave Evil just barely enough power to exist. Its existence literally hung by a hair. It was only man's evil deeds that strengthened it and allowed it to grow.

This is the hair in G-d's Tefillin.

It is the hair of a calf. The Golden Calf is one of archetypes of Evil.

Hair itself is something dead. You can cut your hair and not feel a thing. Yet, it eminates from the living. Its root stems from life.

The same is true of evil. Although it in itself is dead, it ultimately stems from the Source of all life. Nothing can exist without G-d.

G-d's very purpose required the existence of evil. Thus, the hair is right inside His head Tefillin.

But it is only a hair. Evil is only given a hairsbreadth of G-d's life force.

This hair ultimately connects all evil to the Holy. Therefore, it is also the channel through which all evil can be brought back to the Holy and redeemed.

No matter how much evil a man does, G-d's hand is always open to receive him when he repents. When a man returns to G-d, all the evil he has done can be turned to good. [27]

Here again, the Tefillin play a profound role.

The main good that G-d offers us is in a transcendental realm beyond this life. It is where man experiences the closeness to G-d that was His ultimate purpose in creation. This is called *Gan Eden*, Paradise, and the World to Come.

However, for the man who has done evil and remained far from G-d, this is also a time when he must face his Maker. He must experience the burning shame of one who has rebelled against G-d. This burning shame is what we call the fires of *Gehenom*.[28]

The Talmud [29] teaches us that a man who is not utterly sinful experiences *Gehenom* for a mere moment and is then redeemed. This is alluded to in the passage (1 Sam. 2:6), "G-d kills and revives, He brings one down to *Sh-ol*, and brings him up again." It is also the meaning of the verse (Zech. 13:9), "I will bring . . . them through fire, and refine them like silver, and assay them like gold."

This is only true, however, when a person wears Tefillin. The hair of the Tefillin serves as a bond, linking even the evil man to the Holy, and through it he can be redeemed. A sinner who wears Tefillin may descend to *Gehenom*, but he is immediately purified and refined. All the evil he has done can be redeemed and returned to the Holy.

The man who never wears Tefillin does not have this means of redemption.

The Talmud calls him a sinner with his body—the hair binding the material to the spiritual has been broken.

We are taught that the man who does not wear Tefillin cannot escape *Gehenom* unharmed. The Talmud says that "his soul is burned and the ashes scattered under the feet of the righteous," as alluded to in the verse (Malachi 3:21), "And you shall tread upon the wicked, for they shall be ashes under the souls of your feet." They might leave *Gehenom*, but they remain so filled with unredeemed evil that they cannot fully return to the Holy.[30] They do not have this one hair of the Tefillin, and cannot redeem their evil.

This hair therefore remains a lifeline, keeping one in contact with the Holy at all times.

Even if a man sins, as long as he maintains the link of the Tefillin. he can still bring himself back to G-d.

As long as you maintain this hairsbreadth of G-dliness, you can always return. . . .

THE MYSTERY OF TEFILLIN

Now that we have explored some general aspects of Tefillin in depth, we can look at some of its details.[31] As we have already mentioned, every single detail is intimately linked with the very mystery of creation and existence.

In this section, we will present some very deep concepts. But it is important to remember that all this is less than a drop in the ocean of Truth.

The number four is very closely linked with Tefillin. There are four parchments inside four boxes. The shape of Tefillin is a four-sided square. The head Tefillin knot is in the shape of a Dalet, the fourth letter of the Hebrew alphabet. There is an unusual four-headed *Shin* on the head Tefillin.

The number four represents the four stages through which all creation is brought into existance. These are represented by the four letters of the Tetragrammaton, G-d's Name *Yud Kay Vav Kay*. They are: emination, creation, formation, and completion, alluded to in the verse (Isa. 43:7), "All that is called by My Name, for My glory (1), I have created it (2), I have formed it (3), and I have completed it (4)." [32]

We will also come across the number seven, as in the seven windings around the arm. These represent the seven *Midos*, the emanations through which G-d guides the world. They are the seven steps linking G-d to His creation and represented in the seven days of creation. The seven emanations are also represented by the seven branches of the *Menorah*. They are alluded to in the passage (1 Chr. 29:11), "Yours, O G-d, are the greatness (1), the power (2), and the glory (3), the victory (4) and the splendor (5), for all that is in heaven and earth (6); Yours, O G-d, is the Kingdom (7)." [33]

Everything in the Tefillin is made from an animal product. Man is only perfected through his animal nature, that is, through his physical body. Man's main link with G-d is through the physical observance of His commandments.

Everything in Tefillin must be made only from kosher animal products. The physical can be raised to the G-dly only when it is not intermingled with evil.

Tefillin begin with four parchments. These must be perfectly white. This alludes to the Infinite Light at the beginning of creation.

For any creation to exist, this Light had to be modulated and constricted. This is represented by the jet black letters written on the white parchment—"black fire on white fire." [34]

The fact that the letters are intelligent symbols teaches us that this modulation and constriction was through the supernal Intelligence.

The parchments are bound with the hair of a calf. This represents the power of evil, as discussed in the previous section. The very purpose of creation is bound by the necessity of evil in order to give man free will.

Ultimately, G-d's ways are hidden from man. We can sometimes see what G-d does, but only dimly perceive His purpose. The parchments are therefore hidden in a black box.

Scientists sometimes have to deal with a process that they cannot understand. They can, however, measure what goes into this process and what comes out. In such a case, they call this process a "black box." Tefillin are literally such a "black box."

The Tefillin must be square. Our sages teach us that the square is the archetype of that which is man made rather than natural.[35] The ultimate goal depends on man.[36]

The Tefillin boxes must be sewn with the veins of a kosher animal. Our sages teach us that there are 365 main veins in the body, corresponding to the 365 days of the year.[37] The boxes are sewn with twelve stitches, representing the twelve months of the year.[38] A most essential ingredient of creation is time, which makes our world an arena of activity. Only in such a world can G-d's purpose be fulfilled.

The head Tefillin are inscribed with the letter *Shin*. On the right side, it is the usual three-headed *Shin*, while on the left, it contains four heads.

This *Shin* is the first letter of G-d's Name, *Sh-dai*, which is spelled out by the letters of the Tefillin. This Name is associated with channel of G-d's providence *(Yesod)*. The *Shin* on the head Tefillin indicates that G-d's purpose governs all providence.

The two letters *Shin* on the head Tefillin have three and four heads respectively. This gives us a total of seven, representing the seven Midos, or emanations. They appear in letters, intelligent symbols, indicating that we are dealing with the intelligent reason and purpose behind all providence.

In the letter *Shin*, all the heads are connected to a single base. This shows that all forces are ultimately directed toward one goal.[39]

The two straps emanating from the head Tefillin to the right and left represent the two basic forces of creation, love and judgment. While sometimes G-d's love would dictate mercy, His judgment demands retribution. Ultimately, G-d's justice is a combination of the two. This is represented by the knot, binding the two sides together.

The straps are then allowed to dangle to the lower parts of the body. G-d's justice extends to even the lowest levels of creation.

The hand Tefillin are worn on the left arm. The right hand is love and the left is judgment. G-d's love is given freely, but His judgment is dictated by His purpose.

The head Tefillin have four compartments, while the hand Tefillin consist of just one. All four levels of existence are directed toward a single goal.

The hand Tefillin are bound with a knot in the shape of the letter *Yud*. This letter always symbolizes the ultimate good in the World to Come.[40] G-d's action is guided by His ultimate goal which is this Future World.

The *Yud* is also the final letter of the Name *Sh-dai*, the Name associated with G-d's providence. Io-

54

gether with the *Shin* of the head Tefillin, and the *Dalet* of its knot, the Tefillin spell out this Name.

The *Dalet* in the knot represents G-d's justice in all His actions.

The *Yud* represents the final stage, where this justice is expressed in deed.

The seven windings on the arm represent the seven emanations, paralleling the seven days of creation. It is through these seven stages that all things procede from G-d.

The seven rings coiled in a descending spiral represent G-d's ways in guiding His world. They end in three rings around the middle finger, representing the threefold betrothal between G-d and Israel, as discussed in the first section. This betrothal is the goal of the entire process of history. The ultimate betrothal will take place in the Messianic Era and in the World to Come.

FOR GIRLS ONLY

I understand that there may be some girls reading this. They are most probably saying, "All this is very fine. Tefillin are a most wonderful way to bind yourself to G-d. But it is only for boys. Where do we come in?"

On a most simple level, the reason for the commandments is to establish a link with G-d. The most profound way to do this is to resemble Him.

There is one unique way that women resemble G-d in a way that no man could ever hope to. Only a woman can create within her body. Only a woman can bear a child. In this sense, a woman partakes of G-d's attributes more intimately than any man.

The Kabbalists teach us that the hand Tefillin represent the feminine element. The single hollow can be said to represent the womb, and the coils, the umbilical cord.

What man partakes of with an object, woman partakes of with her very body.

The box of Tefillin is called a *Bayis*—literally a house. The woman also has her *Bayis*—the home in which she raises a family. One could say that a woman's home is her Tefillin.

Women resemble G-d through their Tefillin, just as man does through his. The entire world is G-d's house, and the attribute that tends to it is called the *Shechinah* or Divine Presence. It is interesting to note that the word *Shechinah* is of the feminine gender. The Kabbalists call it the *Akeres HaBayis*—literally, the Mistress of the house.

There are two basic elements in Judaism, the home and the synagogue. Unlike other religions where the church is primary, Judaism treats the home and synagogue as being co-equal. Some of our most important rituals belong exclusively to the home, such as the *Seder*, the *Succah*, the Sabbath table, and the Chanukah lamp. The continuity of Judaism rests on the home more than anything else. As our sages teach us, "If there are no lambs, there can be no rams." [41]

This *Bayis*—the home—is a woman's Tefillin. It is her contribution to the overall picture of G-d's purpose.

It is interesting to note that G-d told Moses to Jacob, and teach the sons of Israel." If the Torah does not enter the Jewish home first, there can be no continuity of Judaism.

This spirit of Torah in the Jewish home (*Bayis*) is the same as the parchments of Torah in the Tefillin box (*Bayis*). But this is the domain of the woman.

TEFILLIN IN THE CLASSICS

IN THE TALMUD

Tefillin are Israel's strength. It is written (Deut. 28:10), "And the peoples of the earth shall see that G-d's Name is called upon you, and they shall be awed by you."

Berachos 6a

*   *   *

A man who washes his hands, puts on Tefillin, says the *Sh'ma* and prays is considered to have built an alter and offered sacrifice. He is also said to have truly accepted upon himself the yoke of heaven.

Ibid. 14b, 15a

*   *   *

Rabbi Jeremiah saw that Rabbi Zera was very jubilant. He asked, "Is it not written (Prov. 14:23), 'In seriousness there is profit?' " Rabbi Zera answered, "I rejoice for I have worn Tefillin today."

Ibid. 30b

* * *

Every single Jew is surrounded by seven *Mitzvos.* He has Tefillin on his arm and head, a *Mezuzah* on his door, and four *Tzitzis* on his garment. Thus, King David said (Psalm 119:164), "I will praise You each day with seven."

Tosefta, Berachos 6:31

* * *

A man must constantly touch his Tefillin and not take his mind from them.

Shabbos 12a

* * *

One should be as dedicated in wearing Tefillin as Elisha, the Master of Wings. Once the government issued a decree that anyone wearing Tefillin should be put to death. Elisha defied the decree and publicly wore Tefillin. He was caught by one of the king's agents and captured. They asked him, "What is in your hand." Concealing his Tefillin, he replied, "A dove's wing." When they forced open his hand, they indeed found the wing of a dove in place of his Tefillin. From then on, he was called Elisha, the Master of Wings.

Ibid. 49a

* * *

Many Jews risked their lives in order to wear Tefillin.

Ibid. 130a

*   *   *

It is written (Eccl. 9:8), "Let your garments always be white, and let your head never lack oil." This speaks of the *Tzitzis* and Tefillin.

Ibid. 153a

*   *   *

Man always needs a sign of his bond with G-d. The Sabbath itself is such a sign, but on weekdays, this sign is Tefillin.

Eruvin 96a

*   *   *

One who does not wear Tefillin is counted among those banned by G-d.

Pesachim 113b

*   *   *

Tefillin are called the glory of Israel.

Succah 25a

*   *   *

It is said that Rabbi Yochanan ben Zackai never walked four steps without Tefillin.

Ibid. 42a

*   *   *

Who is a sinner with his body? One who never wears Tefillin.

Rosh HaShanah 17a

*   *   *

The students asked Rabbi Ada ben Ahavah, "Why were you worthy of such long life?" He replied, "One reason is because I always wore Tefillin."

Taanis 20b

*   *   *

Abraham told the King of Sodom (Gen. 14:23), "I will not even take a thread or a shoe strap." Because of this, G-d gave Abraham's children the threads of *Tzitzis* and the straps of Tefillin.

Sotah 44b

*   *   *

The *Mitzvah* of Tefillin encompasses all others.

Kidushin 35a

*   *   *

G-d Himself showed Moses the knot of Tefillin.

Minachos 35b

*   *   *

The knot of the Tefillin is worn at the top, signifying the elevation of Israel. It is toward the body, showing Israel's closeness to G-d.

Ibid.

*   *   *

G-d so loved Israel that He surrounded them with *Mitzvos:* Tefillin on the arm and head, *Tzitzis* on their garment, and a *Mezuzah* on their door.

Ibid. 43b

*   *   *

A man wearing Tefillin on his arm and head, *Tzitzis* on his garment, and a *Mezuzah* on his doorpost, is certain not to sin.

Ibid.

*   *   *

One who does not wear 'Tefillin violates eight commandments.

Ibid. 44a

*   *   *

He who wears Tefillin is worthy of long life.

Ibid.

IN THE MIDRASH

It was a time of religious persecution and a man was being beaten to death. He said, "I defied their ban and risked my life to wear Tefillin. Let me now die doing the will of my heavenly Father."

VaYikra Rabbah 32:1

*   *   *

It is written (Psalms 91:7), "A thousand shall fall at your side . . . it shall not come near you." Through the *Mitzvah* of Tefillin, one is guarded from evil by a thousand angels.

BaMidbar Rabbah 12:3

*   *   *

It is written (Cant. 2:6), "Let His left hand be under my head, and His right hand embrace me."

G-d thus embraces man who wears Tefillin.

Shir HaShirim Rabbah 2:17

*   *   *

It is written (*Ibid.* 4:1), "Behold you are beautiful My love." The beauty of Israel before G-d is Tefillin.

Ibid. 4:1

*   *   *

It is written (*Ibid.* 8:6), "Set Me for a seal on your heart, as a seal on your arm." The Tefillin are this seal of G-d.

Ibid. 8:4

*   *   *

It is written (Ex. 14:29), "And the waters were a wall to their right and to their left." The *Mezuzah* forms a wall to Israel's right, and the Tefillin to their left.

Mechilta ad loc.

*   *   *

Wearing Tefillin is like reading the Torah.

Pesikta Zutrasa, Sh'mos 13

*   *   *

The Jewish people said to G-d, "We would like to immerse ourselves in the Torah day and night, but do not have the time." G-d replied, "Keep the *Mitzvah* of Tefillin, and I will count it as if you spent all your time with My Torah."

Midrash Tehillim 1

*   *   *

The wicked say (Psalms 2:3), "Let us break their bands asunder and cast away their thongs." They "break their bands asunder" and abandon the Tefillin on their arms, and "cast away their thongs," the Tefillin on their heads.

Ibid. 2

* * *

The Messiah will come to give the world *Mitzvos* such as Tefillin.

Ibid. 21

IN THE KABALLAH

Happy is the man who wears Tefillin and fathoms their mystery.

Zohar 1:129a

* * *

When a man wears Tefillin and *Tzitzis,* he enters a realm where the Holy One Himself surrounds him with the mystery of the Highest Faith.

Ibid. 1:140b

* * *

When a man places Tefillin on his arm, he should stretch out his hand as if to draw in the Community of Israel and embrace it with his right arm. Thus, it is written (Cant. 2:6), "Let His left hand be under my head, and His right arm embrace me."

Ibid. 3:55a

* * *

The man who wears Tefillin is crowned as on high. He enters the perfection of Unity, and so resembles his Creator.

Ibid. 3:81a

*   *   *

He who wears Tefillin is called a king on earth, even as G-d is called a King in heaven.

Ibid. 3:169b

*   *   *

Man is bound to the Mother of Israel with two signs, the Tefillin and the Covenant of Abraham.

Tikuney Zohar 7a

*   *   *

When a man wears Tefillin, a voice proclaims to all the angels of the Chariot who watch over prayer, "Give honor to the image of the King, the man who wears Tefillin."

Ibid. 55 (124a)

*   *   *

A man wearing Tefillin is enveloped by the supernal Mind, and the Divine Presence does not depart from him.

Ibid. 69 (159a)

*   *   *

When a man wakes up in the morning and binds himself with the holy mark of Tefillin, four angels greet him as he leaves his door.

Zohar Chadash, Teruman 41b

*   *   *

The Tefillin straps are like chains binding the Evil One.

Tikuney Zohar Chadash 101b

*   *   *

There was a pious man who was very careful about always wearing Tefillin. When he died, the angels on high eulogized him with the verse (Deut. 33:21), "He kept G-d's righteousness and His ordinance with Israel."

Sefer Chasidim 363

WITH THE CHASIDIM

It is told that the saintly Rabbi Levi Yitzchok of Berdichov once saw a simple Jew drop his Tefillin. The man gently lifted them up and lovingly kissed them. The Rabbi then raised his hands and said, "L-rd of the universe: The Jewish people are Your Tefillin. You have dropped them and let them lie on the ground for more than two thousand years, trampled by their enemies. Why do You not pick them up? Why do You not do as much as the most simple Jew? Why?"

*   *   *

It is told in the name of the blessed Baal Shem Tov that the *Mitzvah* of Tefillin is so holy it can bring man to a yearning that will make him depart this world. He must therefore bind them with straps, holding body and soul together.

Sefer Baal Shem Tov, VeEsChanan 83

*   *   *

Rabbi Nachman of Breslov once heard that the saintly Rabbi Levi Yitzchok of Berdichov was forced to wander about. He called his scribe and asked him to examine his Tefillin. He explained that a *Tzadik* like Rabbi Levi Yitzchok is the glory of his generation, and as such, is the Tefillin of the entire Jewish people. If a defect in our people's Tefillin forces him to so wander, all Tefillin must be examined for a blemish.

Yemey Moharnat 28b

*   *   *

G-d desires that we wear Tefillin. Therefore, when we wear them, we are enveloped by His desire. This is true of all other *Mitzvos* as well.

Lekutey Moharan 34:4

*   *   *

Tefillin can help a man master the perfection of speech.

Ibid. 38:1

*   *   *

Tefillin can bring a person to Truth.

Ibid. 47

*   *   *

The light of Tefillin illuminates the holiness of the Land of Israel.

Ibid.

*   *   *

Every day, G-d grants us signs, showing us the way of truth. Through Tefillin you can attain the wisdom to recognize these signs.

Ibid. 54:3

*   *   *

When you overcome evil desires, you break the seal of the Evil One. You are then worthy of the holy seal of Tefillin and the deep insight they provide.

Lekutey Moharan Tanina 5:7

*   *   *

G-d's providence is revealed through Tefillin.

Ibid. 40

*   *   *

The boxes of Tefillin represent wisdom, and the straps, the fear of G-d. You can only bind yourself to wisdom through the fear of G-d.

Ibid. 77

*   *   *

The Tefillin straps encompass your faith, protecting it from the Outside Forces. When your mind and soul are thus safeguarded, you can attain a perception of the innermost Light.

Lekutey Etzos, Tefillin 1

*   *   *

Tefillin are the innermost Light and glory of Israel.

Ibid. 4

*   *   *

Tefillin can bring your thoughts into the World to Come.

Ibid. 5

HOW TEFILLIN ARE MADE

1. The finest Tefillin are made from a single piece of leather. Here we see the first step in the process of making the hand Tefillin. A single piece of leather is pressed over a wooden form.

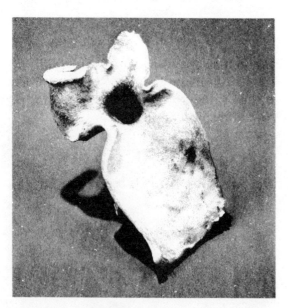

2. Another view of the Tefillin leather after initial forming.

3. The *Bayit* has now been formed and squared. It must be trimmed, smoothed, blackened and sown.

4. A completed *Bayit* of the hand Tefillin. Note the *Yud* shaped knot in the strap.

5. The head Tefillin require a much more complex process. Again, we begin by stretching the leather over a wooden form.

6. The four sections are then formed by stretching the leather over four separate wooden forms.

7. Bottom view of head Tefillin in initial stage. Note that even the four walls of the inner chambers are made of the same piece of leather.

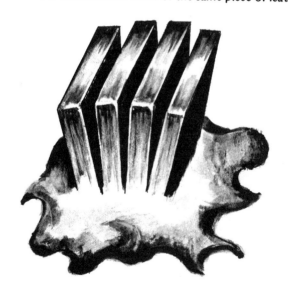

8. The separate sections are then pressed into a squared form.

9. The entire *Bayit* is then placed in a press to give it its final cubic form.

10. The *Bayit* pressed into its final form.

11. Another view of the *Bayit*. Note the four compartments for the four parchments. The *Bayit* must now be trimmed.

12. Pincers are used to draw out the *Shin* on the *Bayit*. The engraved mold illustrated on the lower right is then pressed onto the rough *Shin* to give it a perfect shape. On the right side, this is a usual three headed *Shin*, but on the left, it has four heads. This is the only place where a four-headed *Shin* is ever used.

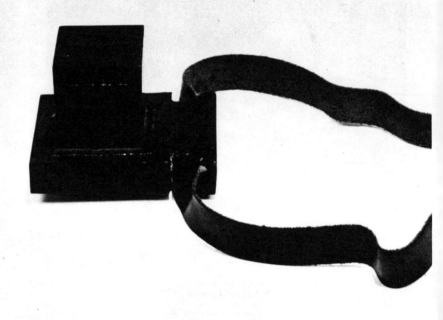

13. A completed *Bayit* of the head Tefillin.

THE KNOTS OF TEFILLIN

Occasions may arise when you may have to replace or adjust the straps (*retzuos*) of your Tefillin. This, of course, is best done by a duly ordained scribe (*Sofer*) or by your rabbi. In some cases, however, you may have to do it yourself.

The most common instance is when you have to loosen or tighten the straps of your head Tefillin to assure a perfect fit. This is shown on Plate 3. The procedure for permanantly fixing the *Yud* shaped knot on the hand Tefillin is shown in Plate 5. Also included is the procedure for making the knots for right handed Tefillin, to be worn by left handed individuals (Plate 7).

If you are replacing the Tefillin straps, it is important to remember that these straps or *retzuos* must be made especially for Tefillin. They should therefore only be purchased from a most reliable source.

Before making any of the knots, you should say, "I am making this knot (*kesher*) especially for the *Mitzvah* of Tefillin."

In an emergency, you may take the straps from one pair of Tefillin and affix them on another. You can similarly transfer the straps from hand Tefillin to those of the head. To reverse this procedure and use the straps from the head Tefillin for that of the hand, however, is forbidden. The head Tefillin have a higher degree of holiness, and this may not be reduced.

A number of pictures here are reproduced or copied from *The Tefillin Handbook,* by Rabbi Shmuel Rubeinstein (New York, 5730) with permission.

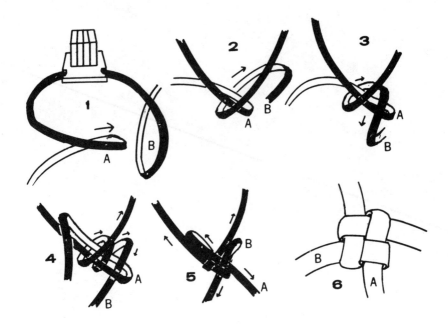

PLATE 1. THE HEAD TEFILLIN KNOT: ASHKENA-ZIC CUSTOM

This plate indicates how to make the Ashkenazic or double *Dalet* type knot, shown in figure 5, page 27.

1. Place the strap through the Tefillin, and center it so that the left side of the strap extends some five inches further down than the right side. (Since the two straps are crossed in the knot, this will result in the right side being somewhat longer than the left.) Then form a loop on each side.
2. Slide the left loop (A) through the right (B).
3. Draw strap (B) through the loop in (A).
4. Loop (B) around, and draw it through the same loop (A) again.
5. Now slip strap (A) over strap (B) and through the loop it forms.
6. Pull both ends tight, and the knot or *Kesher* is complete.

The left hand strap should now reach to your belt, and the right strap a few inches lower. If the strap is too large or small for your head, adjust it according to the instructions on Plate 3.

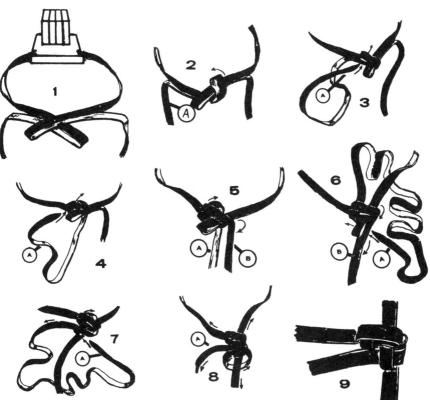

PLATE 2. THE HEAD TEFILLIN KNOT: SEFARDIC CUSTOM

This plate indicates how to make the Sefardic or single *Dalet* knot, shown in figure 6, page 27.

1. Place the strap through the *Ma'abarta* of the Tefillin, and center it so that the right hand strap extends some fourteen inches further than the left. (The straps are not crossed in this type knot, and some eight to ten inches of the right hand side will be used up in making the knot.) Now loop both straps, placing the right loop over the left.

2. Fold the (lower) right loop over the left.

3. Slide the right strap (A) through the loop as shown.

4,5. Repeat this process, drawing strap (A) through the same loop again.

6. Slip strap (A) through lower loop as indicated. Then fold over strap (B) so that it is parallel to that loop.

7,8. Draw strap (A) through the same loop once again, tying down the folded over strap (B).

9. Pull both ends tight. When you put on the Tefillin, the left hand strap should reach your belt, and the right side, a few inches further. If the strap is too tight or loose on your head, adjust according to instructions on plate 3.

79

PLATE 3. ADJUSTING THE HEAD TEFILLIN KNOT

ASHKENAZIC CUSTOM

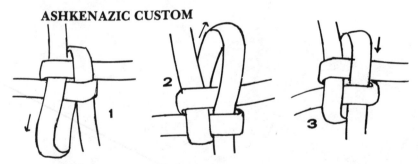

Tightening the head Tefillin.

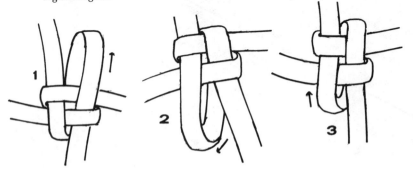

Loosening the head Tefillin.

SEFARDIC CUSTOM

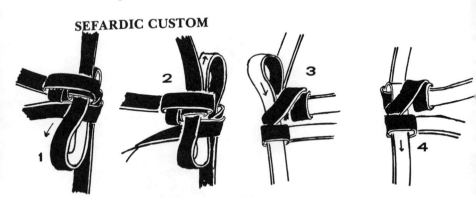

Steps for tightening the head Tefillin. Note that only the right hand strap is made to slide.

To loosen the strap, the exact opposite procedure is followed. The sequence is then 4,3,2,1.

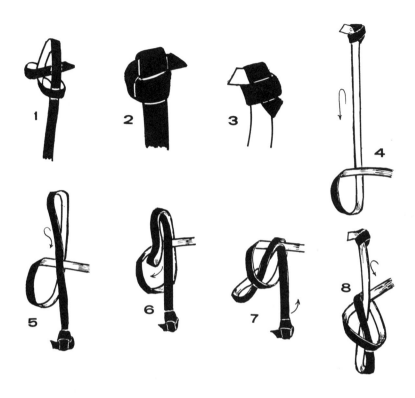

PLATE 4. THE HAND TEFILLIN KNOT: ASHKENA-ZIC CUSTOM

1. The *Yud* shaped knot is made at the very end of the strap. It is actually a simple figure-of-eight knot.
2,3. Front and back views of the *Yud* shaped knot.
4. Make a loop approximately 12 inches from the *Yud* shaped knot.
5. Fold strap down, forming a second loop.
6,7. Fold over top of loop, bringing it through lower loop.
8. You now have a loose slip knot.

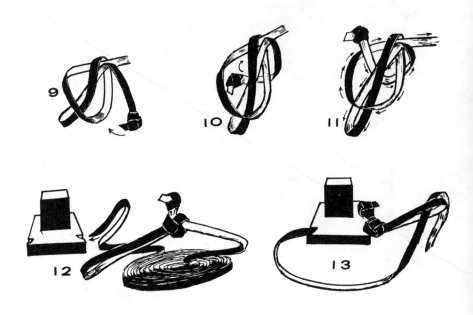

9, 10. Now bring the *Yud* shaped end through the right side of the loop. This stabilizes the knot so that it does not "slip."

11. Tighten the knot as indicated in diagram.

12. Then place the unknotted end of the strap through the *Ma'abarta*, from right to left.

13. Draw strap through *Ma'abarta* until Yud shaped knot is touching the Tefillin box or *Bayis*. Then draw loose end through loop. The Tefillin are now ready to wear. Tefillin made in this manner are meant to be wound *toward* the body.

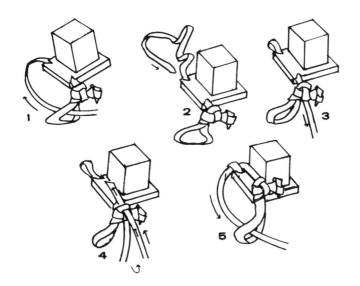

PLATE 5. FIXING *YUD* TO *BAYIS*

The *Yud* shaped knot must always be in contact with the *Bayis* or Tefillin box. In Ashkenazic Tefillin, however, the strap has a tendency to slip, pulling the *Yud* away from the *Bayis*. Here is a procedure often used by *Sofrim* (scribes) to remedy this situation.

1. Remove strap (*retzua*) from loop.
2,3. Pass strap back through the *Ma'abarta* forming a new loop on the left hand side of the Tefillin.
4. Now bring the strap through the top of the Tefillin knot, as indicated.
5. Draw the strap through the new loop on the left hand side of the Tefillin, and pull it tight. This will permanently fix the *Yud* next to the *Bayis*. Then draw the loose end through the loop again.

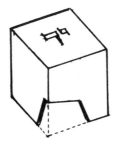

The *Yud* shaped knot should not be separated from the Tefillin even when they are put away. It is therefore customary to cut away the Tefillin cover so that it not separate the two. This is done in the manner shown in this illustration.

PLATE 6. THE HAND TEFILLIN KNOT: SEFARDIC CUSTOM

1. Make *Yud* shaped knot as in figures 1-3, plate 4. Then make a loop approximately 12 inches from this knot.
2. Fold over strap, forming a second loop.
3,4. Fold over top of loop, and draw it through lower loop.
5. You now have a slip knot.
6,7. Now bring *Yud* shaped end through the left side of the loop. This stabilizes the knot so that it does not "slip."
8. Tighten the knot as indicated.
9. Draw the loop through the *Ma'abarta*, and then bring the loose end of the strap through this loop. The Tefillin are now ready to wear. Tefillin made in this manner are meant to be wound *away from* the body.

84

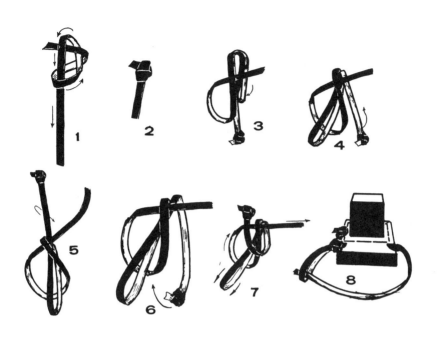

PLATE 7. RIGHT HANDED TEFILLLIN, FOR LEFT HANDED INDIVIDUAL

Tefillin are always worn on the "weaker" hand. A left handed individual must therefore wear Tefillin on his right hand. The knot for such Tefillin must be reversed accordingly.

ASHKENAZIC CUSTOM

1,2. The *Yud* shaped knot is a mirror image of that used in ordinary Tefillin. Instead of pointing to the right, the tip points to the left.

3–5. The slip knot is made as in figures 6–8, plate 4, except that it is a mirror image of that knot.

6,7. The strap is then drawn through the right side of the loop and tightened.

8. The loose side of the strap is then drawn through the *Ma'abarta*, and then through the loop. Note that the Ashkenazic knot for right handed' Tefillin is very much like the Sefardic knot for left handed Tefillin (Plate 6), except that the *Yud* shaped knot is reversed.

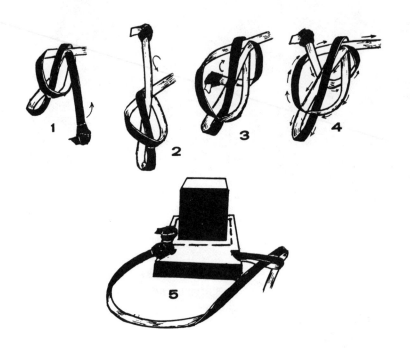

SEFARDIC CUSTOM

1-4. The Yud shaped knot is made as in figures 1,2, above. The knot is otherwise exactly the same as that for Ashkenazic left handed Tefillin, illustrated in plate 4.

5. The loop is then passed through the *Ma'abarta* as shown.

THE LAWS OF TEFILLIN . . .
SOME FINAL QUESTIONS

1. *What is the earliest that Tefillin can be put on in the morning?*

Tefillin can be put on as soon as it begins to get light in the morning. The sky should be light enough so that one can recognize a person's face from about four paces.[1]

2. *What if I do not put on Tefillin in the morning? How late can I put them on?*

You can put on Tefillin all day until sunset.[2] If you have not put on Tefillin until after sunset, you may do so until dark, but without saying the blessings.[3]

3. *What if I do not have Tefillin in the morning?*

You may pray without them, and put them on later when you obtain a pair.

When you put them on later in the day, you should say the Sh'ma or a Psalm.[4]

4. *What if I take the head Tefillin out first?*

You must still put on the hand Tefillin first.[5]

5. *What if I accidently put on the head Tefillin first?*

You need not take it off to put on the hand Tefillin.[6].

6. *What if I accidently talk while putting on Tefillin?*

If you talk between the time you say the blessing over the hand Tefillin and the time you have finished tightening the head Tefillin, you must repeat the entire process. You first loosen the hand Tefillin slightly, say the blessing over it, and then finish putting them on as usual.[7]

If you follow the Sefardic custom and do not usually say a blessing over the head Tefillin, you must do so in case of an interruption. Those who follow this custom, however, need not loosen the hand Tefillin again.[8]

If your talking involved your putting on of Tefillin, you need not repeat the blessing in any case.[9]

7. *What if I only have half a set?*

The hand and head Tefillin are each a separate *Mitzvah,* and therefore, each one may be put on alone.

If you put on the hand Tefillin alone, you say its usual blessing.

If you put on the head Tefillin alone, you must say both blessings.

If you follow the Sefardic custom, however, then you only say the blessing *Al Mitzvas Tefillin.*

The same is true if you have an injury and can only put on one of the pair.[10]

8. *What if I put on Tefillin more than once during the day?*

You must say a blessing each time you put them on.[11]

9. *What if I take may Tefillin off in the middle of the service?*

You need not repeat the blessing when you put them on for the remainder of the service.[12]

If you take them off to go to the bathroom, however, you must repeat the blessings, since it is forbidden to wear Tefillin in the bathroom.[13]

10. *What if I forget to say the blessing when I put on Tefillin?*

You may say them when you remember.[14] It is best, however, to move the Tefillin off to the side a bit before saying the blessing, and then to immediately replace them.[15]

11. *How long must I keep the Tefillin on?*

It is accepted practice to wear them during the entire morning service, until the very end.[16] It is particularly important that they be worn while you say the *Sh'ma* and *Shemonah Esreh*.[17]

12. *What if a strap tears?*

This is a somewhat complex question, and it is best that you consult your rabbi. The following, however, is a general guideline.

If the strap on the hand Tefillin tears, you may say a blessing over it if there is enough strap left to tie the Tefillin in place and wind it three times around the middle finger, even if there is not enough for the windings around the arm.[18] If it is shorter than this, you may put it on without a blessing, as long as there is enough strap left to bind the Tefillin on the arm.[19]

If the strap on the head Tefillin tears, you may put it on with a blessing as long as at least eight inches remains hanging down. If the amount hanging down on either side is shorter than this, you may still put it on, but without a blessing.[20]

In any case, whenever a strap tears, you must get it repaired as soon as possible.

13. *What if the black rubs off or fades from my Tefillin?*

If the black comes off the *Batim* (boxes) you may wear the Tefillin without a blessing.[21]

If the black fades or rubs off the straps, however, the Tefillin become unfit for use.[22] If some black color remains, however, you may wear them without a blessing.[23]

In any case, it is best to consult your rabbi. You should have the Tefillin reblackened as soon as possible, especially where the straps are involved.

14. *What if my Tefillin become damaged?*

Wherever any damage is evident, you must consult your rabbi or a competent scribe.

NOTES ON "WHY TEFILLIN" AND "USING TEFILLIN"
(Pages 11 – 32)

[1] See *Sefer Mitzvos HaGadol (S'mag)*, positive commandments #3; *Orech Chaim* 25:5.

[2] *Lekutey Moharan* 4:6. Cf. *Berachos* 6b, *Shabbos* 30b; Rashi *ad loc.* *"Mitzvos."*

[3] *Kiddushin* 35a.

[4] *Sanhedrin* 88b.

[5] *Sefer HaChinuch* 421; *Yad, Tefillin* 1:3, 3:1.

[6] *Orech Chaim* 32:7.

[7] *Ibid.* 32:3. Cf. *Yerushalmi, Megillah* 1:9 (12a).

[8] *Ibid.* 32:44. The *Yad* and *Sefer HaChinuch* list that the parchments must be wrapped in another blank parchment or cloth. We, however, follow the opinion of the *Rosh*, who states that this is not necessary. See *Magen Avraham* 32:60, *Biur Halachah Ibid. "VeKorachah."*

[9] *Ibid.* 32:39. See *Minachos* 35a.

[10] *Ibid.* 32:42.

[11] *Ibid.* 32:44.

[12] *Ibid.* Here we follow the opinion of the *Shulchan Aruch* which lists the *Titura* and the *Ma'abarta* separately.

[13] *Ibid.* 32:49.

[14] *Ibid.* 33:3.

[15] *Ibid.* 32:52. The Rambam holds that only the *Dalet* is required, but Rashi holds that the *Yud* is also obligatory. See *Biur HaGra ad loc.*, *Shabbos* 62a, Rashi, *Minachos* 35b *"Kesner,"* *Tosefos Ibid. "Elu,"* Mordecai, *Halchos Tefillin.*

[16] *Minachos* 35b.

[17] *Orech Chaim* 39:10, *Mishneh Berurah* 39:28.

[18] *Magen Avraham* 27:12. Cf. *Zohar* 3:228b, *Yad, Tefillin* 3:12.

NOTES ON "A DEEPER LOOK"

(Pages 33 — 58)

[1] *Kiddushin* 35a.

[2] Cf. *Maggid Devarav LeYaakov* #102, *Likutey Monaran* #64.

[3] *Emunos VeDeyos* 1:4 end, 3:0, *Sefer HaYashar* 1, *Pardes Rimonim* 2:6, *Etz Chaim, Shaar HaKellalim* 1, *Reshis Chochmah, Shaar HaTshuvah* #1, *Sh'nei Luchos HaBris, Bais Yisroel* (Jerusalem, 5720) 1:21b, *Shomrei Emunim (HaKadmon)* 2:13, *Derech HaShem* 1:2:1.

[4] *Derech HaShem, Ibid.*

[5] Cf. *Mechilta* on Ex. 14:29, *Berashis Rabbah* 21:5, *Shir HaShirim Rabbah* 1:46; *Yad, Tshuvah* 5:1.

[6] *Berashis Rabbah* 1:2; *Tanchuma, Berashis* 1, *Pirkei DeRabbi Eliezer* 3, *Tana DeVey Eliahu Rabbah* 21, *Zohar* 1:5a, 1:24b, 1:47a, 1:134a, 1:205b, 2:161b, 2:200a, 3:35b, 3:69b, 3:178a, *Bahir* 5.

[7] *Mechilta*, Rashi on Ex. 19:18, *Tanchuma, Yisro* 13; *Berashis Rabbah* 27:1, *Koheles Rabbah* 2:24.

[8] *Tikuney Zohar* 17a.

[9] See *Shaarey Orah* #10, *Pardes Rimonim* 23:20.

[10] See *Maharsha ad loc., Beer HaGolah (Maharal)* #4, *Bechaya* on Ex. 13:16.

[11] *Sh'mos Rabbah* 38:5, *Koheles Rabbah* 1:9, *Sifri, Ekev* 47, *Tana DeVey Eliahu Rabbah* 14, Rashi on Gen. 1:1. Cf. *Berachos* 32b, *Taanis* 3b.

[12] *Berashis Rabbah* 2:1.

[13] *Derech Mitzvosecha (Chabad), Tefillin* #2; *Iyun Yaakov Minachos* 35b (in *Eyen Yaakov* #5). Cf. *Yerushalmi, Sanhedrin* 1:1 (1b), *Tanchuma, Berashis* 5, Rashi on Gen. 1:26.

[14] *Berachos* 7a.

[15] *Yad, Tshuvah* 6:5, *Moreh Nevuchim* 2:48.

[16] See Ralbag, *Metzudos David,* Malbim ad loc., *Yalkut* 2:959. Cf. *Berachos* 55a, Rashi *ad loc.,* "*Terichim,*" *Yalkut* 1:860, 2:306; *Emunos VeDeyos* 4:7 end; Manaratz Chayos, *Megillan* 11a; Radak on Jer. 10:23.

[17] *Emunos VeDeyos* 8:8. Cf. *VaYikra Rabbah* 25:8.

[18] See *Moreh Nevuchim* 3:26.

[19] *Yesod VeShoresh HaAvodah* 2:8.

[20] See *Amud HaAvodah, Hakdamah Gedolah* #31; Rabbi Yitzchok Ashlag, *Hakdaman LeSefer HaZohar* (in *Sulam*) #9; *Idem., Talmud Eser Sefiros, Histaklus P'nimis,* part 1, 1:4 (p. 15).

[21] See Rabbi Moshe Chaim Lutzatto, *Pischey Chochmah VoDaas* #3.

[22] *Likutey Amarim (Tanya)* 1:4, *Likutey Moharan* 33:4, 34:4.

[23] *Orech Chaim* 32:44.

[24] Cf. *Midrash Tehillim* 36:4, *Zohar* 1:23a, 2:184a, *Akedas Yitzchok* 70 (3:145b), *Etz Chaim, Shaar HaMelachim* 5, *Sefer Baal Shem Tov, Sh'mos* #9.

[25] *Chulin* 60b.

[26] *Zohar* 3:47b.

[27] *Yoma* 86b.

[28] *Ikkarim* 4:33, *Nishmas Chaim* 1:13. See my article, "On Immortality and the Soul," in *Intercom* 13:2 (Sivan, 5732).

[29] *Rosh HaShanah* 17a.

[30] Ramban, *Toras HaAdam, Shaar HaGamul, "VeAchshav,"* (Jerusalem, 5715) p. 78a.

[31] See *Shemonah Shaarim, Shaar HaKavanos, Inyan Tefillin; Shaar Maamarey Rashbi* (Ashlag, Jerusalem, 5721) p. 273 ff.; *Pri Etz Chaim, Shaar HaTefillin; Shnei Luchos HaBris, Mesechta Chulin* 1:185b, *Derech Mitzvosecha (Chabad)* p. 16b ff., *Likutey Halachos (Breslov), Hi lchos Tefillin.*

[32] In a Kabbalistic sense, these are the four worlds, *Atzilus, Beriah, Yetzirah* and *Asiyah,* being respectively the worlds of *Sefiros,* souls, angels and the physical.

[33] These are the last seven of the Ten *Sefiros.* The first three denote mental activity, and the last seven, action.

[34] *Yerushalmi, Shekalim* 6:1 (25b), *Shir HaShirim Rabbah* 5:9, *Zohar* 2:84a, 2:114a, 2:226b, 3:132a, 3:154b, *Tikuney Zohar* 56 (90b).

[35] *Yerushalmi, Nedarim* 3:2 (9a).

[36] See *Bahir* 114, *Elema Rabosai* (Ramak) 1:4:14 (29b).

[37] *Zohar* 1:170b, Targum J. on Gen. 1:27, *Makkos* 24a.

[38] *Orech Chaim* 32:51.

[39] *Bahir* 81.

[40] *Minachos* 29b, Rashi on Gen. 2:4.

[41] *Yerushalmi, Sanhedrin* 10:2, *Berashis Rabbah* 24:3, *VaYikra Rabbah* 11:7, Rashi on Isa. 8:18.

NOTES ON "THE LAWS OF TEFILLIN."

[1] *Schulchan Aruch, Orech Chaim* 30:1.
[2] *Orech Chaim* 30:2. See *Mishnah Berurah* 37:6.
[3] *Pri Megadim, Eshel Avraham* 30:7, *Mishnah Berurah* 30:3.
[4] *Mishnah Berurah* 58:5.
[5] *Orech Chaim* 25:6.
[6] *Shaarey Tshuvah* 25:10, *Mishnah Berurah* 25:22; *Tshuvos Yaabatz* 125, *Shiurey Brachah* 25.
[7] *Orech Chaim* 25:9, *Magen Avrham,* 25:15, *Mishneh Berurah,* 25:32.
[8] *Ibid.*
[9] *Orech Chaim,* 25:10.
[10] *Orech Chaim,* 26:1.2.
[11] *Orech Chaim,* 26:12.
[12] *Ibid. in Hagah.*
[13] *Magen Avraham* 25:22.
[14] *Pri Megadim, Eshel Avraham* 25:12, *Mishnah Berurah* 25:26.
[15] *Cf. Magen Avraham* 25:15.
[16] *Orech Chaim* 25:13.
[17] *Orech Chaim* 25:4.
[18] *Orech Chaim,* 27:8, *Mishnah Berurah,* 27:44.
[19] *Magen David* 33:6, *Chayay Adam* 14:8.
[20] *Mishnah Berurah* 27:44.
[21] *Mishnah Berurah* 32:184.
[22] *Biur Halacha* 33:3 *"Retzuos."*
[23] *Ibid. "Retzuos" #2.*